A Claude Monet Painting
`A Young Woman Sitting`

By

Virgil Haverstick

A Claude Monet Painting

'A Young Woman Sitting'

Copyright © 2018 by Virgil Haverstick

Specialty Art LLC.

All rights reserved. This book or any portion thereof may not be reproduced or used in any manner whatsoever without the express written permission of the publisher except for the use of brief quotations in a book review.

Dedication

II

This book is dedicated to my wife Cathy. In the thousands of days in my life, the most important was and always will be the day we met.

To Jim Beveridge for his friendship and unwaivering support all these years and lastly in memory of my Dad, Virgil Haverstick *(5/11/1922- 11/22/2005)*

Table of Contents

Chapter 1:	pg	5	Introduction
Chapter 2:	pg	6	Comparisons
Chapter 3:	pg	17	The Mc Crone Report
Chapter 4:	pg	32	Brushstrokes - The use of Paints
Chapter 5:	pg	46	Monet's Sketchbook
Chapter 6:	pg	50	Monet's Account Books -Auction
Chapter 7:	pg	58	The Provenance
Chapter 8	pg	63	Conclusion

Summary

Ch 1 <u>Introduction.</u>   A missing painting `A Young Woman Sitting'

Ch 2 <u>Comparisons</u>   Comparisons to other painting Monet did of Camille.

Ch 3 <u>The McCrone Report</u> The test of the paint to compaireto Monets pallette and the mixing of colors as Monet.

Ch 4 <u>Brushstrokes</u> The use paints – Brushstrokes – Colors – Comparisons.

Ch 5 <u>Monets Sketchbook</u> A sketch in book #1 pg. #1, that went with Monet to Holland that has similarities to our painting. Both painting & sketch with dates of 1871.

Ch 6   <u>Monets Account books & Auction</u>   Records that lead to a missing painting.

Ch 7 <u>The Provenance</u> – A complete history of the painting

Ch 8 <u>Conclusion</u> This book provides evidence that this is the discovered and missing painting Claude Monet sold at auction 1873 `A Young Woman Sitting'

Chapter 1

The Drouot Auction records show that on Febuary 4th 1873 Claude Monet sold a painting to gallery owner Paul Durand-Ruel. Their records list the paintings name as `Jeune Femme Assise' or `Young Woman Sitting.' Paul Durand-Ruel records list the painting as `Femme Assise' or `Woman Sitting.' The Durand-Ruel records record the purchase but the sale is missing.

Around 100 years later Daniel Wildenstein found that missing painting ` Young Woman Sitting' and renamed it `A Young Woman Sitting'
In his 1974 Catalogue Raisonne of Claude Monets painting he renamed it once more when he summited it into the provenance of the painting `Springtime.'

By 1980 he changed his mind. The painting 'A Young Woman Sitting' is not in `Springtimes' provenance when he published his 1996 Catalogue Raisonne. Therefore the painting once again became a missing painting.

My name is Virgil Haverstick Jr.
It is my pleasure to present to you the missing painting,
`A Young Woman Sitting.'   By Claude Monet.

My father Virgil Haverstick Sr. bought the painting from another family by the name Wildenstein. [No connection to Daniel Wildenstein, the famous art family or the Wildenstein Institute.] What attracted my father to the painting was the french impressionist style, and later the resemblence of the painting to other paintings Monet did of his wife Camille.

Chapter 2
COMPARISONS

Camille-Leonie Doncieux (1847- 1879), Claude Monet's first wife. Camille posed for many paintings that are famous today.

Here is our painting. Please compare it to other paintings Monet did of Camille.

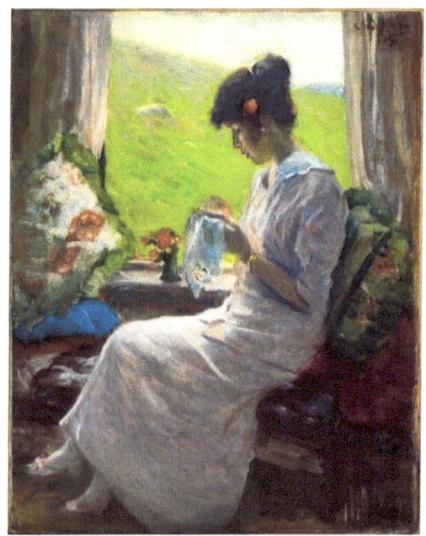

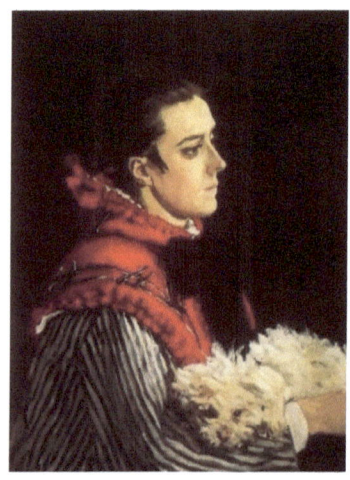

Camille with a small dog, 1866

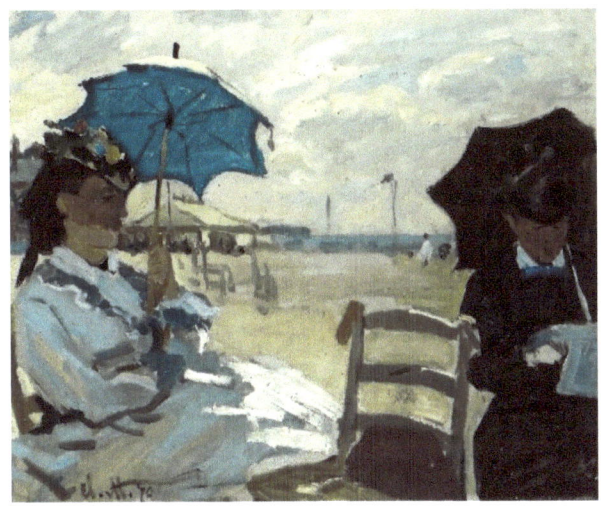

The Beach at Trouville, 1870

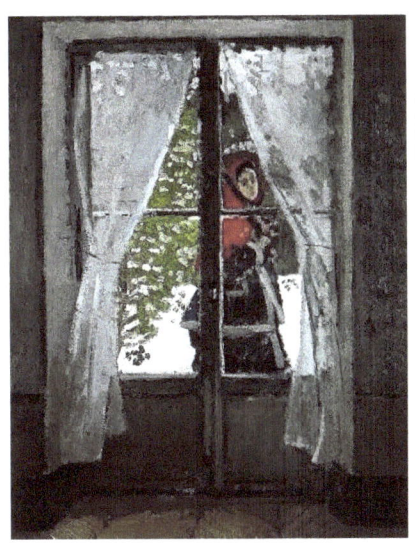

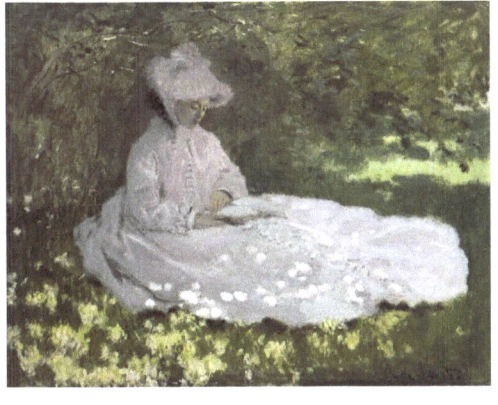

Springtime, 1872

The Red Kerchief, 1873

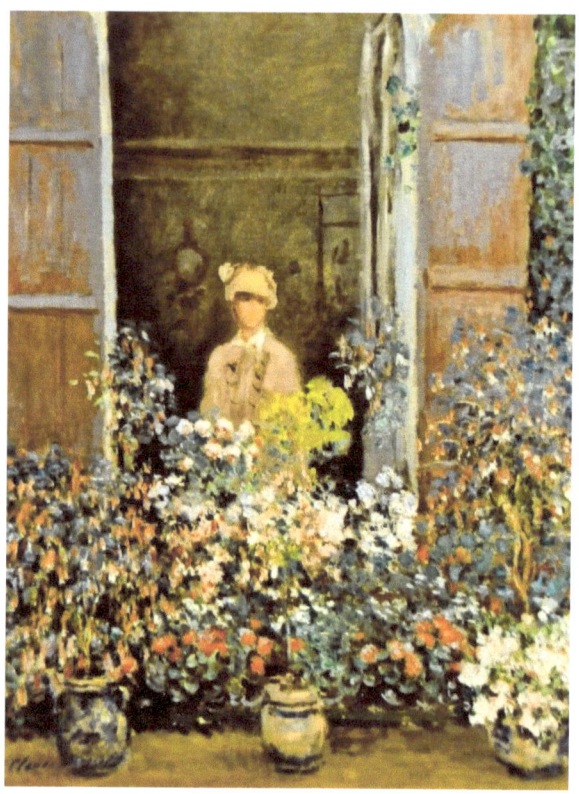

Camille Monet at a Window, 1873

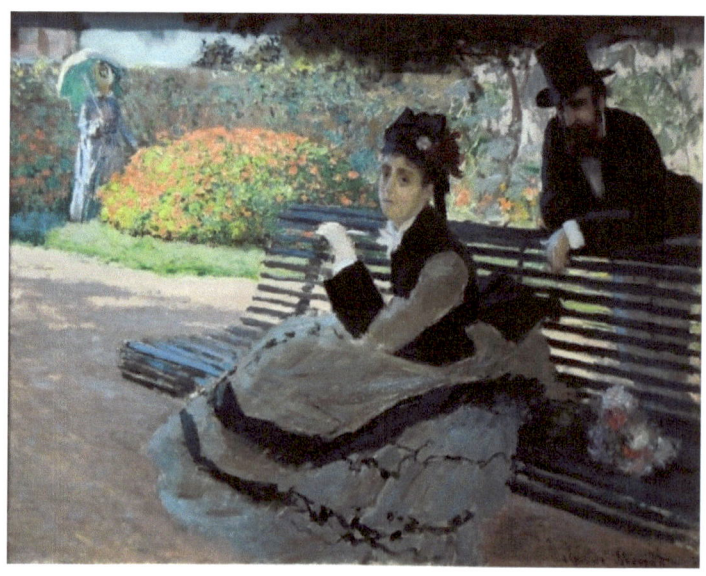

The Bench, 1875

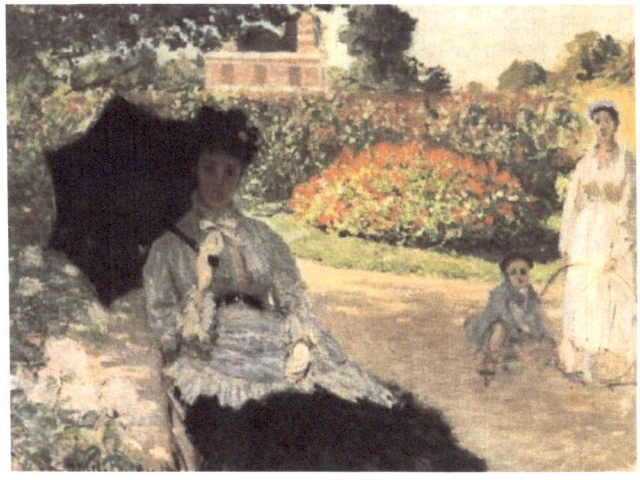

Camille in the Garden with Jean and his Nanny, 1873

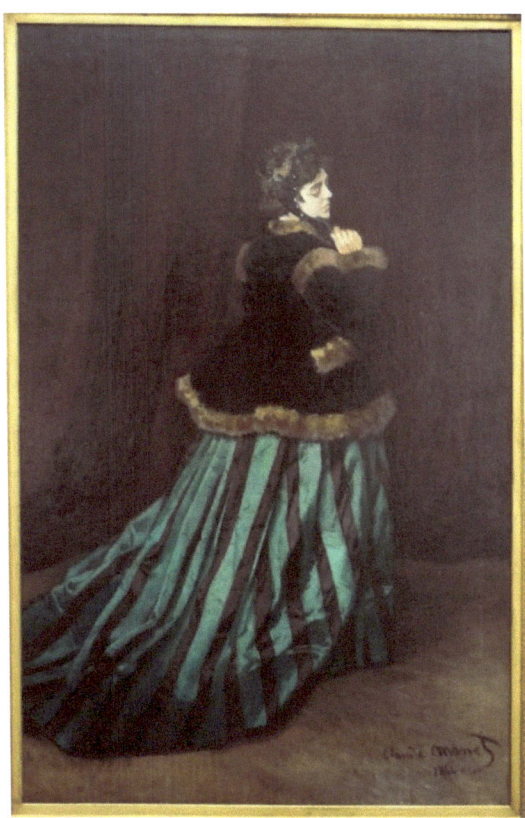

The Woman in the Green Dress, 1866

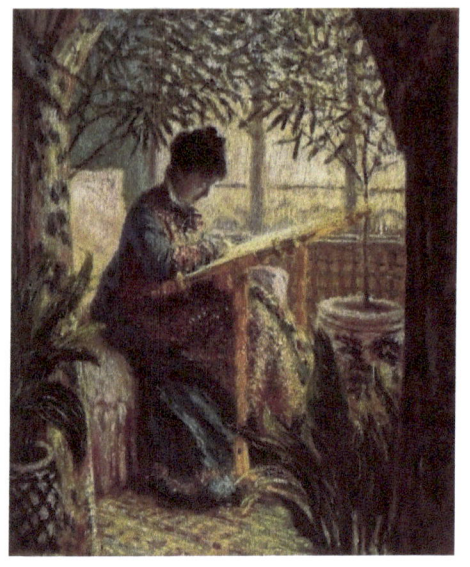

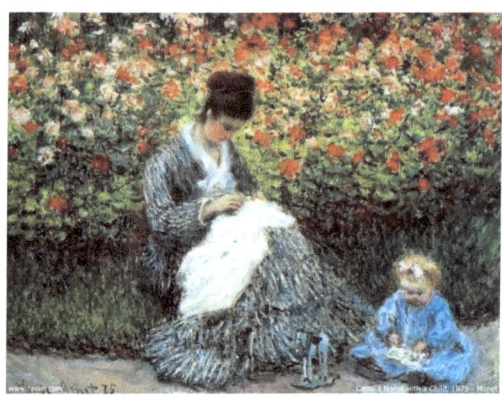

Camille Monet and a child in the Garden, 1875

Madame Monet Embroidering, 1875

Camille was still in her teens when she met Monet in 1865. She was of humble origins and worked as a model. She was an attractive, intelligent girl with dark hair and beautiful eyes. Camille soon became Monet's girlfriend, mistress and model. The couple lived in depressing poverty. Camille and Monet were married in 1870 and had two sons: Jean and Michael born in 1867 and 1878, respectively.

Like the wives of other great Impressionistic painters, Camille was virtually lost in the shadow of the man whose life she shared. For as much as Monet may have possessed his genius and resolved to struggle to the top of his art form, the woman who remained at his side must receive her well-deserved recognition not only because she posed for many of his inspired works, but because she shared his miseries, hopes and disappointments. Throughout many years of suffering and uncertainty, she dutifully inspired and supported his work.

While viewing each of these paintings, we notice that the most noticeable feature is how different the paintings seem. Monet painted Camille within a 12-year period, thus capturing her inevitable changes in physicality throughout the years. As a result, these paintings of Camille clearly reflect Monet's evolutionary changes which corresponded with the introduction of Impressionism.

Compare our painting to some of Monet's other works which featured Camille:

- Age of Camille
- Health of Camille
- The use of similar props such as couch, sewing, etc.
- The same use of hair
- The body language (the head, neck, posture)
- The same face (nose, mouth, lips)
- Monet's use of color (red's, blue's, yellow's, and red spots)
- The same use of reflective light and shadows
- The use of white dresses and flowing gowns
- The painting of Camille's face in realism and the rest of the painting impressionism
- All paintings of Camille have subtle differences; however, each is unique unto itself

Compare these two paintings:

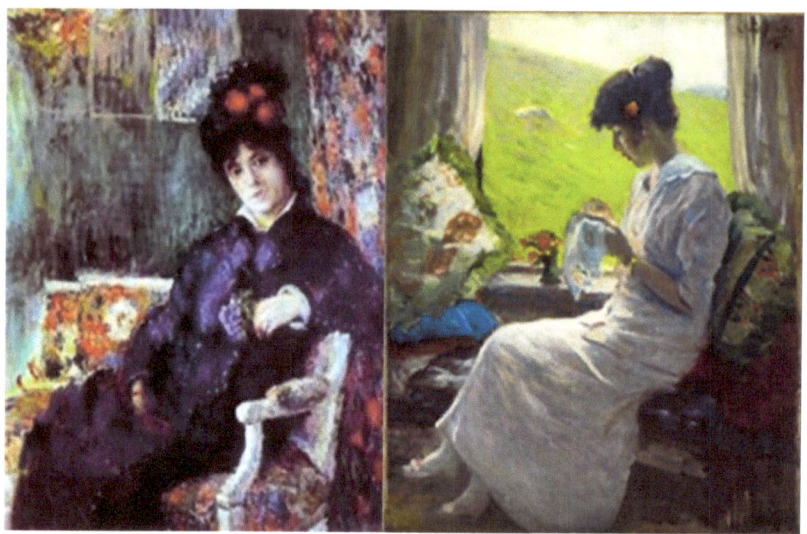

Camille Holding a Posey of Violets

- An object in her hands
- Sitting on a couch
- Flowers
- Use of curtains
- Notice the same structure of the face, the nose, the protruding lips, the hair worn up, and the distinguishing posture of her neck and head.
- There is an age difference of approximately six to ten years to take into consideration here.
- The same background

Daniel Wildenstein gives us a way to identify Camille in a Claude Monet painting, "The pictures in which she appears are easily recognizable by the lick of hair that hung down her cheek."

In our painting, we clearly see the 'lick of hair that hangs down her cheek', distinguishing her as Camille.

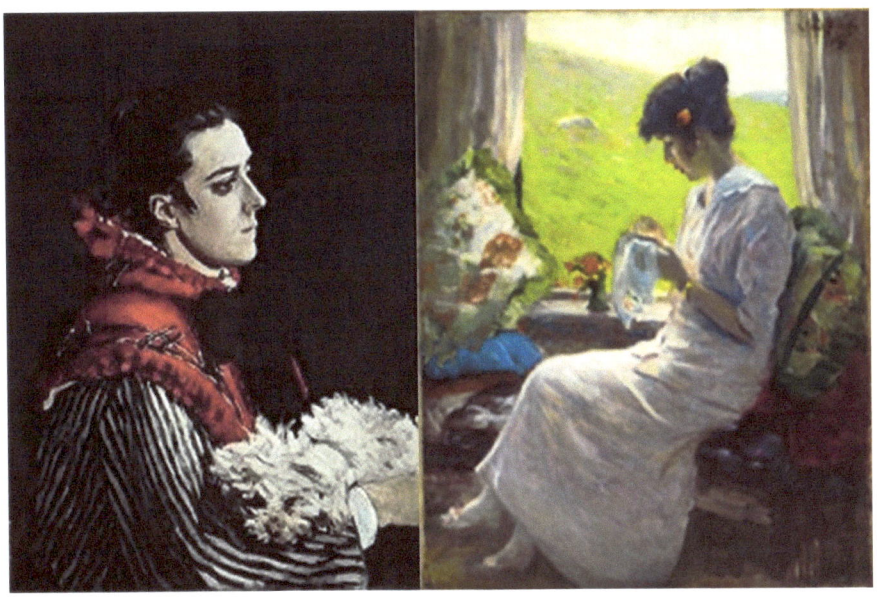

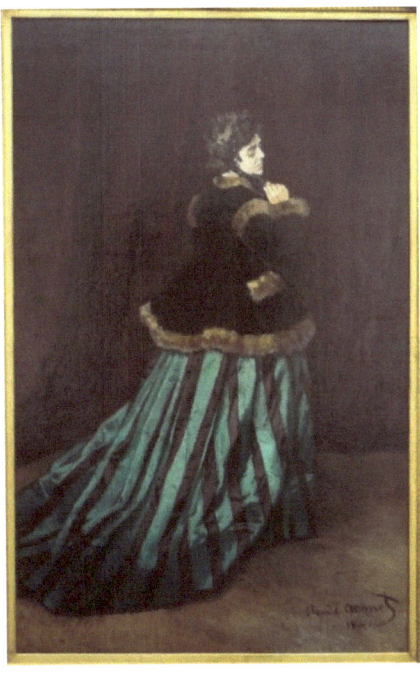

Monet did the painting named 'Meditation, Mrs. Monet sitting on a Sofa.' Compare the hands of both paintings, the forming of the hands are the same and both are hi-lighted the same. Both painting dated 1871, one painted in London the other in Holland.

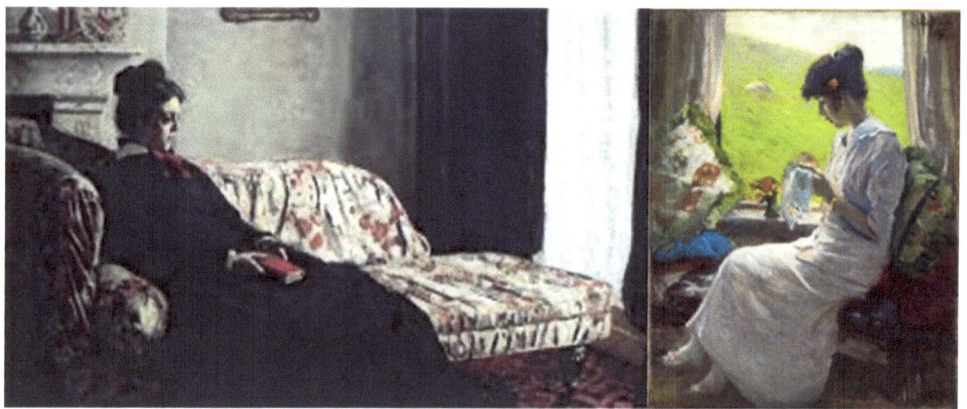

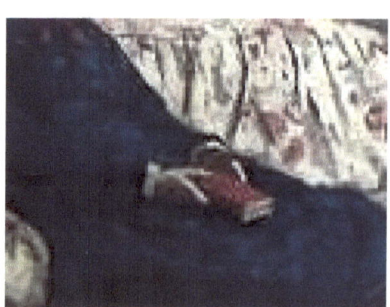
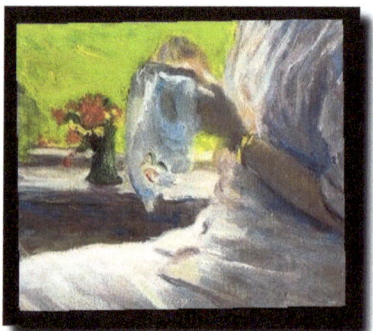

Also look at Madame Monet in Japanese Guise - 1876 and Camille and Child - 1875. One is an Impressionist painting and the other is Realism.

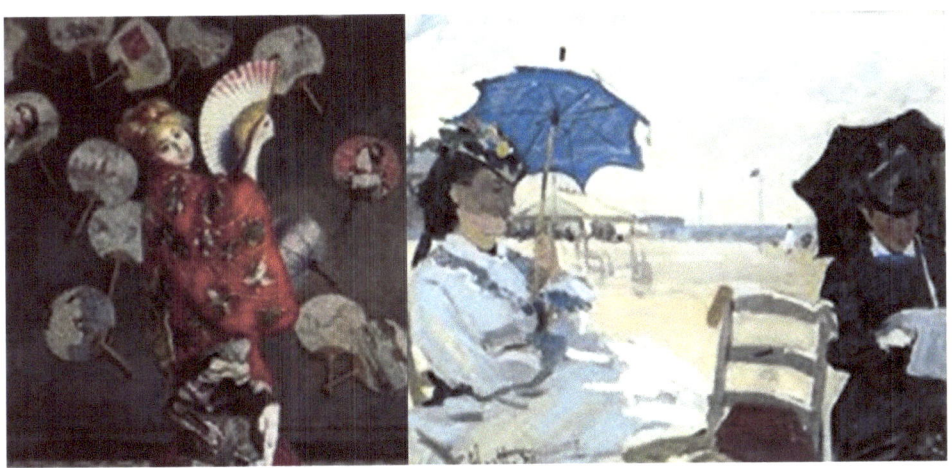

Among the paintings of Camille, there are many additional comparisons however, most of them have to do with the degrees of Realism and Impressionism, the differences in age, health, and of course the various ways in which an artist can interpret the model in that particular setting or mood.

Camille and Child – 1875. Here, it is easy to compare the same posture, the neck, the hands, as well as the hair.

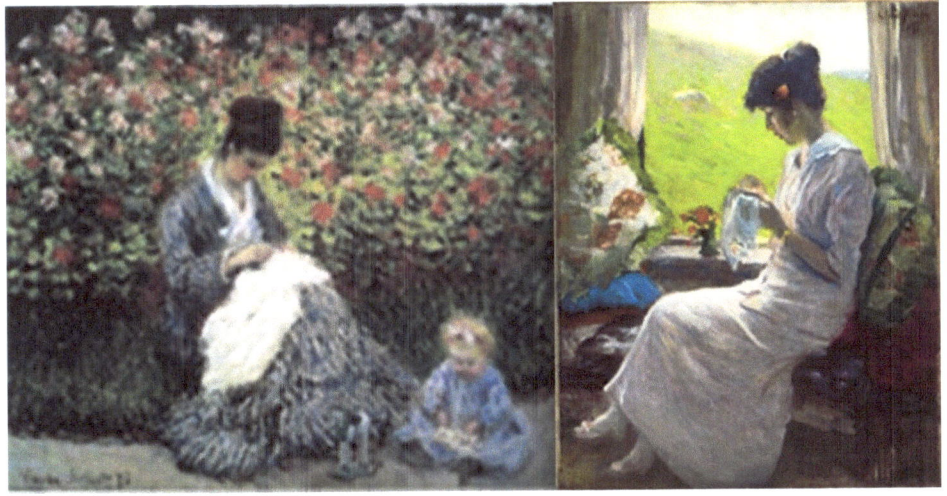

Compare our painting to a drawing Monet did of Camille in about 1868 named "Portrait of a Woman". They have the same mouth, nose and cheeks.

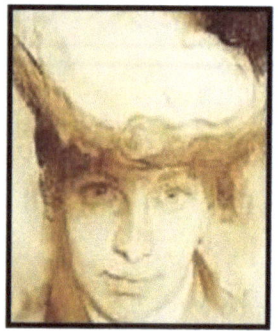 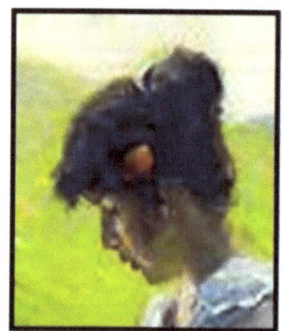

Chapter 3
The McCrone Institute Report

Scientific Authentication takes place from esteemed Dr. Walter McCrone of the McCrone Institute and Dr. Ashok Roy from The National Gallery, London.

After the painting remained in storage for many years, Dad decided that he was ready to have it tested for authentication. From there, he searched for the best scientists in the world and chose someone with an impeccable reputation and international recognition; Walter McCrone of the McCrone Research Institute in Chicago, Illinois.

The McCrone Research Institute is an Illinois based, not-for-profit Corporation that is dedicated to teaching, research and applied microscopy. Founded by Walter McCrone in 1960, the McCrone Research Institute (McRI) was organized in order to fill a technical and scientific gap. Though the light microscope is a valuable analytical tool, few universities in the world properly teach its use and application. However, the McCrone Research Institute meets this need.

<u>Here are a few highlights of Dr. McCrone's significant achievements throughout his career:</u>

1974 - Dr. Mc Crone was involved in the Vinland Map which was found to be a fake.

1978 - Dr. McCrone worked on The Shroud of Turin.

1980-1990s - Dr. McCrone was involved in Old Masters painting authenticity with artists such as Manet, Monet, Rembrandt, Da Vinci, Picasso and others.

Few scientists have bibliographies as extensive or as respectable as that of Dr. Walter C. McCrone. He was never motivated by profit and openly shared knowledge with his competitors as he regarded them as students, or disciples of microscopy. McCrone would meet privately with students before the start of 8 a.m. classes and on weekends. He traveled extensively, giving hundreds of lectures and was always willing to write an article at the behest of a journal editor, or teach a specialized discovered microscopy course for a particular company, college or field of study. We sought after the best in working with Dr. McCrone, and he enlisted the best in Dr. Ashok Roy, the Director of Scientific Research at the National Gallery in London.

Since 1977, Dr. Ashok Roy has worked on a technical examination of the old masters paintings and was a principal contributor to five of the *Art in the Making* exhibition series, and editor of the National Gallery Technical Bulletin. Since 1978, Dr. Roy's research interests have centered upon the study of old master paintings by scientific methods, as well as the history and technology of painting methods and materials of which he has widely published.

The National Gallery founded in 1824, houses the British national collection of Western European paintings with approximately 2400 works which span from the 13th to the early 20th centuries.

The art is on display 361 days out of the year, free of charge. This collection of Western European paintings throughout the 13th to the 19th centuries is one of the greatest in the world, and receives nearly 4.5 million visitors per year. Each of its 19 departments cover a wide range of activities which include the care, preservation, study, presentation and promotion of the collection, educational activities and visitor services.

Their scientific department is a world leader regarding its technical study and meticulous handling of their collection, as well as providing multidisciplinary research alongside the conservation and curatorial departments. Particular areas of expertise include: the analysis of the materials of paintings, the history, technology and development of European painting techniques and materials, as well as the literature of painting practice.

Within conservation science, their strengths are in preventive conservation, monitoring and environmental management of picture galleries, and the assessment and monitoring of additional factors which are potentially damaging to the art (such as shock and vibration within buildings, and for paintings traveling on loan).

In addition, studies are undertaken to examine the deterioration of traditional painting materials (fading, darkening, chemical interaction and so on), the factors responsible, and also the safety and reliability of conservation procedures for paintings, particularly with respect to cleaning.

The scientific department has also established a leading presence in the field of high-resolution digital imaging of paintings for accurate color recording and has conducted research in digital archiving and access to technical documents on works of art.

The NGL is involved and responsible for the activities aimed at defining the best practices and protocols towards common standards and is also involved in the trend's National Access Program (ARCHLAB), along with outreach programs created to enhance scientific activity. The NGL fosters the implementation of a portal to cultural heritage, knowledge and the development of innovative methodologies and instrumentation for Dr. Walter McCrone was a leader in the fields of optical microscopy, crystallography, ultramicroanalysis, and particle identification for over 50 years. He was born in Wilmington, Delaware on June 9, 1916, but grew up primarily in the state of New York. After completing his undergraduate degree in chemistry, followed by a graduate degree in 1942 at Cornell University, McCrone began his two years of postdoctoral research in chemistry, specializing in chemical microscopy. In 1944, he joined the Armour Research Foundation (now known as the Illinois Institute of Technology Research Institute), where he developed and supervised the analytical chemistry department and became the assistant chairman of that department.

McCrone founded McCrone Associates in 1956 as an organization dedicated to research in microscopy, ultramicroanalysis, and crystallography. The goal of the program was to apply the most modern methods available to hone the complex tools of optical and electron microscopy in order to solve many problems of both government and industry. Over the years, McCrone Associates has grown from a one man/one microscope facility to an internationally recognized research institute, serving more than 2000 clients each year.

In 1960, McCrone founded the McCrone Research Institute of Chicago; a non-profit corporation devoted to fundamental research and teaching of optical and electron microscopy and crystallography. Over the past forty years, the Institute has hosted over 20,000 students in all facets of microscopy, and has been expanded to include McCrone Scientific, a sister organization headquartered in London, England. The McCrone Research Institute remains one of the prominent centers of excellence for microscopy in the world.

During the course of his 60-year career in microscopy, Dr. McCrone published over 600 technical articles, including 16 books. He was the editor and publisher of the international applied journal in microscopy, *The Microscope* for over 30 years. Originally launched by Arthur Barron in 1937, this scientific journal is dedicated to the advancement of all forms of microscopy for the biologist, mineralogist, metallographer and chemist. The journal publishes original, previously unpublished works from the microscopical community and serves as the proceedings of the *Inter/Micro* microscopy symposia held in Chicago each year. It emphasizes new advances in microscope design, new accessories, new techniques, and unique applications for the study of fibers, particles, films, and surfaces of all materials, whether inorganic, organic or biological. McCrone's best known publication, *The Particle Atlas*, appeared in a six-volume second edition from 1973-1979 with an updated CD-ROM version in 1992. This particular work is recognized as one of the best handbooks available for solving material analysis problems.

McCrone's acclaimed work with the Shroud of Turin received worldwide attention in 1978 when he concluded that the Turin Shroud is a medieval painting. This observation was vindicated by radioactive carbon-14 dating techniques in 1988. In 2000, McCrone received the American Chemical Society National Award in Analytical Chemistry for his work on the Turin Shroud and for his enduring patience in defense of his work for nearly 20 years.

During his remarkable career, McCrone has received many honors and awards. At the invitation of the American Chemical Society, McCrone lectured for over 50 years on various topics in microscopy. In 1979, McCrone retired as active president of McCrone Associates in order to research and teach on a full-time basis.

A Protocol for the Authentication of Paintings

By Walter C. McCrone and Eugene Markowski

The art world recognizes the need for organization when charged with the task of evaluating the claims of authenticated artist paintings. If this panel states that the evidence of shown to experts has sufficiently proved the likelihood that a given painting is authentic, then their published conclusion should be accepted and validated by the art world.

My interest in authenticating stems from 30 years of studying paintings scientifically. This includes pigment, medium and support identification using polarized light microscopy, flourier transform infrared absorption, energy dispersive x-ray analysis, infrared and ultraviolet light examination, x-radiography and when helpful, dendrochronology and carbon dating. These methods enable us to evaluate attribution of the painting to a particular artist. I always recommend these scientific tests be done first because they are far less costly than the investigations of provenance, iconography, style, etc. and because 80% of the paintings I have studied fail the scientific tests and the useless expensive connoisseur studies are avoided (unless the owner wishes to establish a different attribution).

I have reported the 20% of paintings I've passed using my scientific tests to possibly be correctly attributed. I've usually stated that I found no scientific result to render the attribution false. I occasionally feel pretty sure the attribution is correct.

Still, no collector whose painting has passed my tests has been able to gain acceptance of their attribution by the scholars. Many have spent years and many dollars in further investigations without encouragement, much less success and sale. Their paintings are in limbo. There is unfortunately little mutual understanding or respect between the scientists and the scholars. My thinking has now evolved to think of the need for a group, hopefully IFAR, to finally bring the authentication studies of both scientists and scholars to a mutual conclusion that will eventually be accepted by the art world, and the world of limbo may then lose some of its many inhabitants.

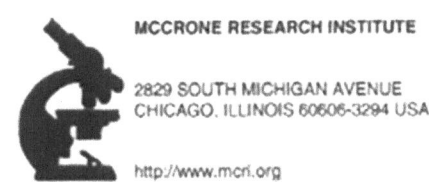

MCCRONE RESEARCH INSTITUTE

2829 SOUTH MICHIGAN AVENUE
CHICAGO, ILLINOIS 60606-3294 USA

http://www.mcri.org

2 March 2000

From: Walter C. McCrone

Subject: Painting attributed to Claude Monet

Dear sirs,

I have finally finished our study of the 45 x 55.5 cm painting attributed to Claude Monet (1840-1926). Eleven samples were taken, mounted in Aroclor®, a standard refractive index medium for characterization and identification of pigments by polarized light microscopy. A Scanning Electron Microscope with Energy Dispersive Detector (SEM/EDS) was used to obtain supplemental chemical analyses.

The pigments thus identified in this painting, with their dates of first use, were lead white (ancient), viridian (1825), chrome yellow (1818), lemon yellow (1809), ultramarine (ancient), cerulean blue (1805), burnt sienna (ancient), zinc white (ancient), and madder (ancient). All of these pigments were available to Monet; in fact, all of them were used by Monet in this painting. His palette is well known as a result of studies by Dr. Askok Ray at the National Gallery in London*.

The samples with their locations follow:

1. Ground (white)   3-3/4" from right edge along top edge.
2. Light blue   6-1/4" from right edge along top edge.
3. Brown (Signature)   3/4" from top, 1/4" from right edge.
4. Green   10-1/2" from top, 2" from right edge.
5. Red brown   7 3/4" from bottom, 1/4" from right edge.
6. Gray-green   along bottom edge, 5-1/2" from left edge.
7. Gray   along bottom edge, 5" from left edge.
8. Blue   along left edge, 9" from bottom edge.
9. Red   11-1/2" from bottom edge, 5-1/2" from left ed
10. Yellow   12" from bottom edge, 7" from left edge.
11. White   5" from bottom edce, 3" from left edge.

*National gallery Technical Bulletin, Vol. 9 (1985) pp. 12-20

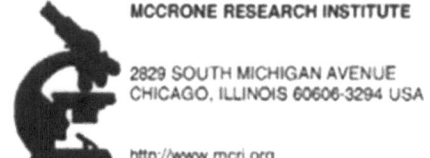

MCCRONE RESEARCH INSTITUTE

2829 SOUTH MICHIGAN AVENUE
CHICAGO, ILLINOIS 60606-3294 USA

http://www.mcri.org

2.

Sample	Pigments
1.	Lead white
2.	Viridian, zinc white
3.	Burnt sienna
4.	Viridian
5.	Lead white, zinc white, madder, cerulean blue
6.	Lead white, viridian
7.	Zinc white, viridian, ultramarine (trace)
8.	Lead white, cerulean blue, ultramarine
9.	Burnt sienna, cerulean blue, ultramarine, viridian
10.	Chrome yellow, barium chromate (lemon yellow) Zinc white

Everything we have seen and done agree remarkably well with the known palette of Claude Monet. I see no reason to doubt the attribution to one of my favorite artists, Claude Monet.

Yours sincerely,

Walter C. McCrone

WCM:aj
Enc

After his study of our painting, Dr. McCrone concluded that the analysis of pigment sample agree remarkably well with the known palette of Claude Monet. **Therefore, the McCrone Institute concluded that our painting was indeed an original Claude Monet painting.** Dr. McCrone utilized the McCrone Institute along with Dr. Roy's resources at the National Gallery in London and was able to draw the conclusion based on more than just the study of paint samples.

Dr. Roy's report in the Technical Bulletin volume 9 begins with a reference to bulletin volume 5, and samples which were taken of Monet's painting, *Bathers at La Grenouillere*. He makes mention in part of the new pigments, along with oil paint contained in collapsible tubes in which pigment and medium were ready mixed. It is apparent from the cross-sections, as well as from the swirls of color in the paint surface, that the technique was at least partly wet-in-wet with some mixing carried out on the canvas. This method is consistent with sketchy and rapid paintings in the open. Moreover, the pigment mixtures involved in some of the colors, especially Monet's greens, are fairly complex.

Volume 9, *The Palettes of Three Impressionists Paintings* is a study of Monet's *Gare Saint-Lazare,* Renoir's *La Yole*, and Cezanne's *Mountains in Provence.* Monet and Renoir paintings are close in date; Cezanne's is painted at a later date. The paint is of the 19th century pigments, but there are striking differences in the manner of painting and in the use of color. In his painting, *Gare Saint-Lazare* Monet applied paint, wet-in-wet, on a pure white or off-white ground with some mixing of paint on the surface. Whereas Renoir used pure color, often containing only a single pigment or tent. Monet's paints are a complicated mixture of disparate pigments.

Referring to several techniques and the specific brushstrokes that Monet used, Dr. McCrone drew from these techniques in order to compare them to our painting. Dr. McCrone concludes in this report that the paint used in our picture was applied wet into wet on a pure white or off-white ground [canvas] with some mixing of paint on the canvas. Just like Monet's other paintings, *Bather at La Grenouillere* and *Gare Saint-Lazare,* our painting uses complicated mixtures of disparate pigments.

On page 2 and paragraph 4 in bulletin 9, the most common mixture of colors is some combination of cobalt and cerulean blue, emerald green and viridian, red lake and vermillion, all mixed with a little white. Dr. McCrone took 11 samples from our painting; all are mixed with lead white and/or zinc white. Monet used light-colored ground [canvas] as a device to intensify the overall luminosity of the scene. The canvas used in our painting is light-colored or gray. Scientific research by men such as Dr. McCrone, and Dr. Roy should be used to highlight comparisons and to help prove authenticity.

View the technical bulletin volume index. This is a complete list of 33 volumes from 1977 to 2012

<u>http://www.nationalgallery.org.uk/technical-bulletin/technical-bulletin-volume-index</u>

Dr. McCrone confidently extended a rare sentence in his report stating, *"Everything we have seen and done agree remarkably well with the known palette of Claude Monet. I see no reason to doubt the attribution to one of my favorite artists, Claude Monet."*

<u>Technical Bulletin volume 9 states that, "Monet's paintings are a complicated Mixture of disparate Pigments,</u> while Renoir for the most part painted straight out of the tube."

Here is the comparison of the complex mixing of differing shades of green pigments in the background of our painting dated 1871:

The pigments identified in our painting, with their corresponding dates of first use:

Lead White – Ancient

Viridian Green – 1825

Chrome Yellow – 1818

Lemon Yellow – 1809

Ultramarine – Ancient

Cerulean-Blue – 1805

Burnt Sienna – Ancient

Zinc White – Ancient

Matter Lake – Ancient

Below is a list of the mixing of pigments which Dr. McCrone found from the 11 samples taken from our painting:

The Mixing of 4 Pigments:

[2 Samples]

- Lead White, Zinc White, Madder, Cerulean Blue
- Burnt Sienna, Cerulean Blue, Ultramarine, Viridian

The Mixing of 3 Pigments:

[3 Samples]

- Zinc White, Viridian, Ultramarine
- Lead White, Cerulean Blue, Ultramarine
- Chrome Yellow, Lemon Yellow, Zinc White

The Mixing of 2 Pigments:

[2 Samples]

- Viridian, Zinc White
- Lead White, Viridian

No Mixing of Pigments, stright out of the tube

[4 Samples]

- Lead White
- Burst Sienna
- Viridian
- Zinc White

The paint used in our painting, fits in well with other paintings from 1869 -1877

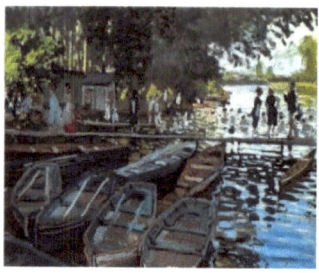 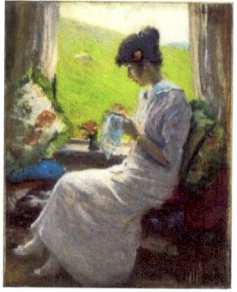 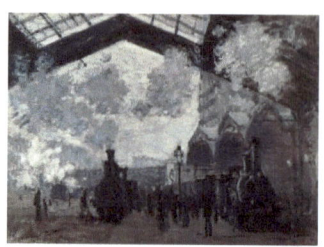

1869	1871	1877
Bathers at La Grenouillere	A Young Woman Sitting	La GareSaint-Lazare
National Gallery, London	McCrone Research Institute	National Gallery, London
Lead White – Ancient	Lead White-Ancient	Lead White-Ancient
Viridian Green – 1825	Viridian Green-1825	Viridian Green 1825
Chrome Yellow – 1818	Chrome Yellow-1818	Chrome Yellow
Lemon Yellow – 1809	Lemon Yellow-1809	
	Ultramarine-Ancient	Ultramarine-Ancient
	Cerulean Blue-1805	Cerulean Blue
	Burnt Sienna- Ancient	
	Zinc White-Ancient	
	Madder Lake-Ancient	
Vermillion red		Vermillion Red
Cobalt Violet		Cobalt Violet
Persian Blue		Persian Blue
Cobalt Blue		Cobalt Blue
Emerald Green		
		Red Alzarin Lake
		Black (Probably)
Chrome Greem		

The McCrone report consisted of the identification of pigments, the use of brushstrokes, the wet into wet mixing of colors, as well as the thorough examination of the canvas itself. Dr. McCrone confirmed that all qualities of our painting matched those of Claude Monet's artwork and even asked to borrow our painting in order to use it as an <u>instructional tool</u> for his students several months after reporting his findings, stating that, "Not many paintings like this come to the institute." Our painting also passed the paint analysis tests: the manner of painting and the use of color at the National Gallery, London.

In the National Gallery, London - Technical Bulletin No. 28 in 2007, Dr. Roy opens with the following passage:

"The national gallery possesses two large canvas paintings by Claude Monet: *Water Lilies and Irises.* Both were painted in his studio at Giverny. Towards the latter part of his career, Monet changed his palette and method of painting and began to paint more simply, and on a much larger scale than in his earlier work. At the same time, he appeared to have restricted his palette to materials, which he believed would generate the better survival of his paintings. For this reason, he abandoned chrome yellow pigments [with the exception of zinc chromate yellow], and consistently used cadmium yellows instead. He took up cobalt violet [cobalt arsenate] and no longer used emerald green [copper acetoarsenite], only employing viridian for his later works. These changes in materials and methods for Monet's pre-20th century work are described."

In Volume 28, Dr. Roy identified 5 pigments from our painting that were still used by Monet, in 1917

1. Lemon Yellow
2. Ultramarine
3. Viridian
4. Lead White
5. Matter Lake

Monet discontinued the use of 4 pigments, from our painting, between 1871 - 1917

1. Burnt Sienna – He used for the signature
2. Cerulean Blue – Now, he could afford the more expense pigments
3. Chrome Yellow – Toxic Color
4. Zinc White – He favored Lead White

Monet added 5 pigments within this 45-year span, 1871 - 1917

1. Cobalt Violet
2. Cobalt Blue
3. Cadmium Orange
4. Cadmium Yellow
5. Vermillion

Comparison: Pigments used in our painting 1871 *
<u>Claude Monet pallet in 1917 / Renoir Pallet in 1919</u>

1. Lead white * / Lead White *
2. Cobalt Blue
3. Ultramarine * / Ultramarine *
4. Viridian * / Viridian *
5. Colbart blue / Colbart blue
6. Cadmium orange / Emerald green
7. Zinc/chromate(lemon)yellow * / Naples yellow
8. Cadmium yellow / Chrome yellow *
9. Rose Madder Lake * / Alizarin Crimson (synthetic Madder lake) *
10. Vermillion / Vermillion

Can you imagine the excitement that my father felt? For the first time in 30 years he had proof that his suspicions were correct, having finally received confirmation that the painting he owned was indeed an original, signed Claude Monet. His excitement was palpable at that time, and he expected the art world would be enthusiastic as well.

After all, Dr. McCrone stated that 80 percent of all paintings within his 30 years of study had failed scientifically, leaving only 20 percent with the possibility of correct attribution.

When the painting was picked up he noticed our carrying case and chuckled. He pointed to a pile of very expensive pouches that had been left behind by disappointed owners of paintings that had failed the authentication process. "Take your pick!" he said.

Virgil Sr.'s exhilaration would be short-lived however, as he approached the major auction houses, he was informed that scientific proof was not enough to be accepted into their auctions. He was told that they, "had a process in place" in which the Wildenstein Institute must declare that our painting was a Monet.

It was at about this time that I was personally becoming more involved, and it was becoming apparent how little we understood about the politics of the art world. None of us had ever heard of the Wildenstein Institute, but that would soon change. We were told that we would be required to furnish the provenance of the painting and were advised that presenting 'comparisons' of our painting to other Monet paintings would help our case. I could see the auction houses and collectors point of view, it seemed reasonable to me.

Throughout the next chapter you will see and be able to compare our painting to Monets use of paints and how he mixed and applied colors.

Chapter 4
Brushstrokes – The Use of Paints

I studied Dr. McCone's Report along with Dr Roy's Technical Bulletins # 5 and 9 that are at The National Gallery in London. They are readily available. I encourage you to read them to see how Dr. McCrone came to his conclusion. He saw that our painting compares to Monet's mixing of colors and the use of his brushstrokes to form his famous Wet-into-Wet, technique. He found that Monet was going through an evolution of style within this period, and many books have been written on this subject, a few of which I will list.

***Claude Monet*, written by William "Bill" Seitz (William C. Seitz)** - In 1960-1970, William Seitz was the Professor of Modern Art History at Princeton University, and Curator of the Department of Paintings and Sculpture Exhibit - Museum of Modern Art, New York. In 1970, he became the William R. Cannon Jr. Professor of Art at the University of Virginia, and the 1972-73 Kress Professor at the National Gallery of Art, Washington DC.

A excerpt from his book, *Claude Monet*

"Monet, changes style numerous times, thickness rhythm of brushstrokes very according to the subject and he would put in influences of artists who he admired, like Diaz and some paintings Doughigny Troycon and Corot (p. 21). He also had problems with visualization and interpretation in his changing from realism to what we know as Impressionism. So he painted in many styles, especially from 1863 to 1875. In London in 1871, he was inspired by Turner the English artist (p. 24). He even followed artists Whistler, Boudin, Jongkind and Colbert and Manet."

Seitz continues, "It would be hazardous to list the characteristics of Monet style during this period. Unlike a studio landscapist, who inevitably repeats his own mannerisms, he was led by variations in light, atmosphere and season, to marked differences in treatment from motif to motif. These in turn qualified both by underlining trend of his evolution and by subjective factors that are hard to evaluate (p. 25-26). Several of the English paintings of the 1871, for example are loosely constructed, yet Westminster Bridge grayed and simplified by the fog, is geometric, and its flat tones are precisely stepped. Many of the Dutch studies of 1871-72 are freely handled; the picturesque shapes of windmills, sails and rowing figures are laid in with little detail, in broad, relaxed strokes".

In this change of his styles from 1863- 1875 was the real birth of Impressionism and how he used so many styles. You really cannot 100% differentiate one from the other as you can see with the painting *On the Beach , Trouville.*

Seitz further explains that, "It is not easy to suggest or even fully to comprehend the variety of Monet's work and his immense productivity. Concurrent with the more famous cycles of 1889-1901 he completed, in addition to uncounted one of a kind works, several other series. Among them are winter landscapes painted outdoors in Norway, in which he employed a broad style recalling that of the 70s."

Here are a few excerpts from, *The Impressionists at First Hand,* published by Thames and Hudson, London 1987, reprinted 1991
"Monet while in London (1871) achieved a looser technique and greater lightness of color. Monet's style was in total change while he was in London- influenced by visiting museums seeing works by Turner, Constable. Monet and Pizarro were trying to improve the use of light from Turner and Constable. Monet took all this influence with him to Holland and surprises friends by his range and variety" (p. 104).

"Monet employed a higher keyed palette, [sometimes using new chemically derived pigment of greater intensity] more contrast and a flatter application all of which gave greater separateness to his painted marks then was the case with Constable" (p. 2).

Techniques of the Great Masters of Art, by Quantum Books

"His colors, like his ready-made prepared canvasses, were bought ready-made". Pg 172

The canvas and stretcher bars of our painting were purchased ready-made.

"The 1860s was a decade of dynamic change in painting". Pg 118

"Monet had a Technique called mixing or wet-into-wet, which is to add oil to paints and mixing colors on the canvas, but this sometimes darkened a painting. On the other hand, removing oil from paints to achieve the 'dragging effect' causes other problems. The ideal consistency varies from pigment to pigment."pg. 156

"Along with grinding, oil and additives, paintings were given a layer of Bitumen which is a varnish or sealer. When first applied Bitumen gives a seductive warm transparent brown, but Bitumen is a tarry substance, akin to asphalt used for resurfacing roads today, and consequently, it never dries completely. Its subsequent cracking and blistering in fluctuating environmental temperatures destroys the paint surface, while the color blackens, losing transparency as it ages." Pg 122

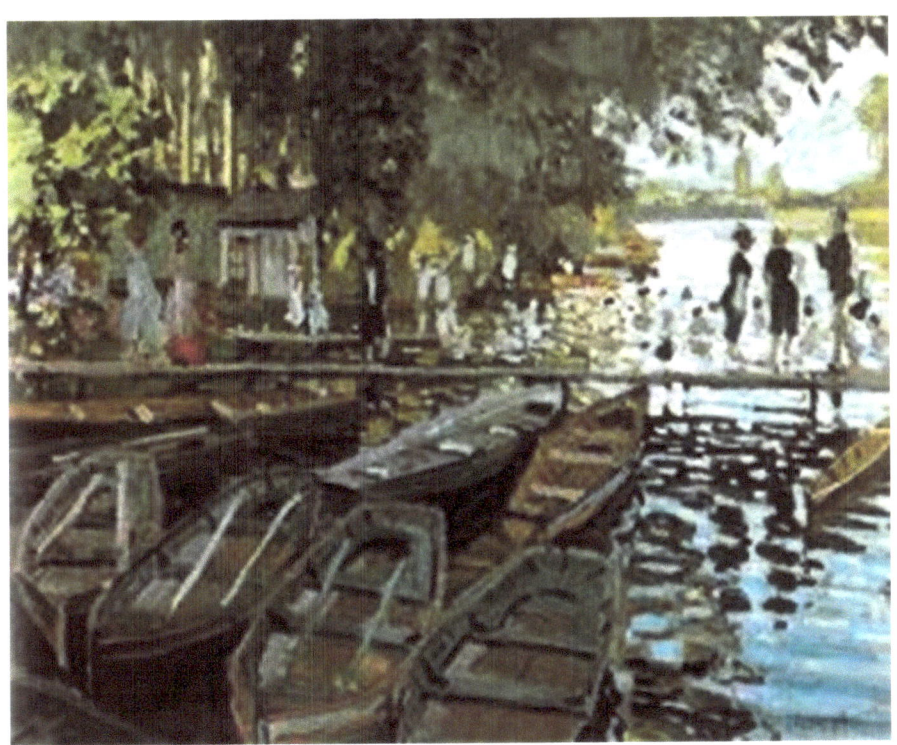

Bathing at Grenouillere

Monet's painting, Bathing at La Grenouillere - 1869 is mentioned in Techniques of the Great Masters of Art. A letter from Monet to his friend and artist, Frederick Brazil on September 25, 1869, when he was working at La Grenouillere, makes it clear that Monet was still working in the traditional manner; seeing studies like this as preparatory works for potentially larger studio created works. In this painting, Monet's brushwork is vigorous and the individual and distinguishable brush marks indicate that hog's hair brushes between about 1 - 2 cm. wide were used. There is little variation between the size of the stroke in the foreground and background to suggest depth, although more uniformly straight horizon all strokes and pastel shades on the distant water aid the impression of depth and recession. His brushstroke is strongly deceptive, catching character of different forms long, unbroken strokes outline the boats, short horizontal dabs indicated for groundwater, abrupt jabs are used for flowers and foliage. Monet rejected traditional, smooth brushwork, which created an illusion of surface texture instead, hurried handling helps to invoke the actual natural textures Monet's talent for summarizing the essential character of his landscape is already apparent in his early characters, which demand an ability to capture basic feature concisely. Pg 154-156

Continuing from Techniques of the Great Masters of Art, in his paintings from the 1870s on, lead white was liberally used in most of his color mixtures, bringing with it a new overall brilliance and pale pastel like quality, as he sought to depict the light tones and mental light and dark contrasts of full sunlight landscapes. "Monet combined slurred wet-in-wet mixing on the canvas with free mixed use, for example, the somber colors on the boats are obtained by mixing complementary colors, like red and green, which gives darkish neutral hues that are more colorful than those made by sullying a color with black." Pg.156

Our painting follows the dialogue in this article quite nicely as it exhibits some of the traditional manners of painting, as in the wet-in-wet, and the use of brushwork in the background. The article states that Monet's brushwork is vigorous and it indicates that Hog's hair brushes between 1-2 cm were used. This can be seen in the background of our painting as well as the mixing of the light green and dark green mixed with yellows. Examining the McCrone report, it also matches this article's description of Monet's use of lead white in the 1870s which was liberally used in most of his color mixtures. This again is exactly the case in our painting, which brought out its overall brilliance. The changing of Monet's style was evident between this 1869 painting Bathing at the Grenouillere and our 1871 painting. As referenced earlier, the changes in Monet's use of paints and brushstrokes are well documented by William Seitz's book, Claude Monet and by other authors.

1869 is now commonly seen as a turning point in the development of the Impressionist style. Although their method and palette was to change considerably within the following decade, the basis for the Impressionist technique was already well established.

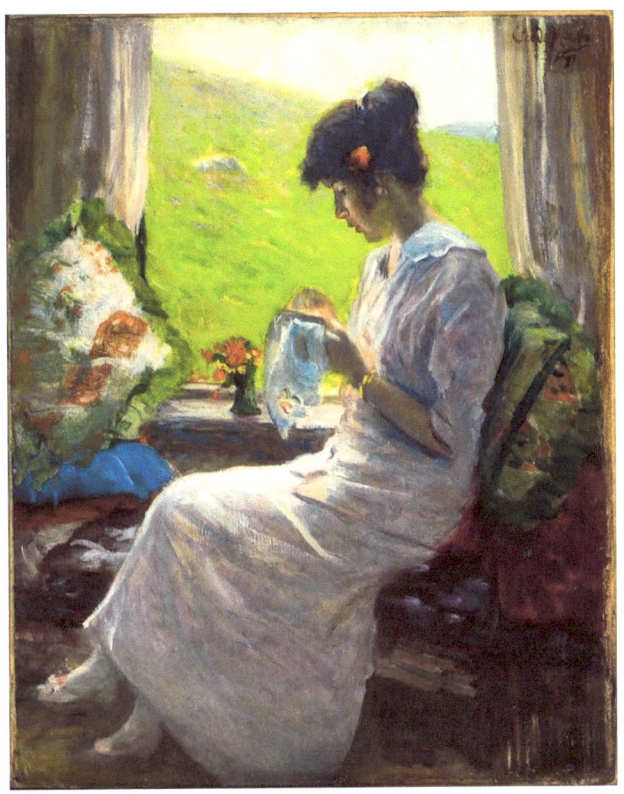

Monet's style of applying paint, wet-over-dry has also been identified in our painting. Please examine Camille's dress. You will see the wet-in-wet technique as well as the view outside of the window. Notice the 'multiple mixing of colors' (dark greens light greens and yellows) and the dragging of dry stiff paint across the surface. This is shown in the outlying of Camille's dress from her lap to the hem of her dress.

The Impressionists were experimenting with new paints at this time. The styles of, wet-in-wet and the dragging and multiple mixing of colors required them to learn the use of thinners and thickeners. The brown sauce bitumen and the improper balance of oils and waxes resulted in the cracking and darkening of paint.

***Nature into Art* by John House**

"Claude Monet spoke of his innovations in color of the mid-to-late 1860s. He said in 1900; 'I was still far from having adopted the principles of 'division of colors' which turned so many people against me, but I was beginning to experiment with it in part, and I was, working at effects of light and color at which ran counter to accepted convictions" (p. 111).

Professor House continues, "These comments show that he was consciously pursuing unconventional ways of translating his visual experiences into colour. His interest in the *rayon* and the *reflect* echoes Delacroix's Dieppe notes, and the 'principle of the division of colours' is what Silvestre had described in Delacroix's works. Delacroix expressed this even more clearly in one of his notebooks. 'Constable says that the superiority of the green in the field derives from the fact that it is made up of a multitude of different greens. The reason why the greenery of most landscapists lacks intensity and life is that they usually treat it in one single tint. What he says here about the green in the medals can be applied to other hues" (p. 111).

When Claude Monet produced our painting he was still developing into what we know today as a great Impressionist artist. The latter 1860s into the early 1970s are the years that led to what we know of him today. Our painting depicts him as he experimented with the division of colors that professor House spoke of in his book.

Claude Monet's use of the technique, 'slurred wet-into-wet', 'mixing on the canvas', 'dragging', the principles of 'division of colors', and liberal mixing of white with pigments are all collectively corralled in Dr. McCrone's report, the McCrone Institute and the studies at the National Gallery, London from Dr. Ashok Roy (see also chapter four of John House's book, (*Monet Nature into Art*). Dr. Roy's technical bulletin, volume 9 mentions the wet-into-wet, mixing of colors and his report references Monet's painting *Gare Saint-Lazare* and a list of pigments, which coincidently are all mixed with white pigments.

Dr. McCrone took 11 samples from our painting. Once again, you can see that our painting adheres to Monet's technique; the mixing of white pigments with other colors.

Pigments Mixed with White in our Painting

The Mixing of 4 Pigments:
[2 Samples]
- **Lead White**, **Zinc White**, Madder, Cerulean Blue
- Burnt Sienna, Cerulean Blue, Ultramarine, Viridian

The Mixing of 3 Pigments:
[3 Samples]
- **Zinc White**, Viridian, Ultramarine
- **Lead White**, Cerulean Blue, Ultramarine
- Chrome Yellow, Lemon Yellow, **Zinc White**

The Mixing of 2 Pigments:
[2 Samples]

- Viridian, **Zinc White**
- **Lead White**, Viridia

No Mixing of Pigments:

[4 Samples]
- **Lead White**
- Burst Sienna
- Viridian
- **Zinc White**

Revolution in Paint **by Perry Hurt**

"By the first Impressionist exhibition in 1874, there had been 200 years of government control of the arts in France through the French Academy, which perpetrated humanist artistic traditions established 300 years earlier, during the Renaissance, including the painter's palette of pigments had barely changed in 400 years. It was time for a revolution. Pg.1

Young painters, including Claude Monet, Alfred Sicily, and Camille Pizarro shared frustration over the confining of academic painting. Influenced by a few maverick painters that preceded them, and inspired by an unprecedented number of newly invented paint pigments, these artists invented a new style that we call 'Impressionism'."

"The birth of modern science and the Industrial Revolution in the 18th century Europe supplied an unprecedented expansion in the artist's palette. More than 20 intense yellow, green, blue, red, and orange pigments were invented between 1800 and 1870. The Impressionist took advantage of the new pigments inherent chromatic and physical properties to forgo the look laborious techniques of traditional academic painting for a quicker and more direct painting style. These innovations, and the new paint tube, helped the impressionists seize the flickering light, and pulsing life around them, abandoning the conservative historical and mythological studio products of academic painting."

"Today the prismatic colors, impasto, and quick summary style of impressionist paintings receives nearly universal praise, but when first established in the 1870s the reaction of the public and many critics was quite the opposite. A comparison of the materials and painting techniques of the academic painters and the Impressionists will help to remind us of the radical and unconventional nature of a new school of painting that would survive the harsh criticism of its day and come to captivate a world audience."

"Thus the battle really is between traditional art and the new art, between old painting, and the new painting." - Edmond Duranty, 1876 pg. 1

"Some people burst out laughing at the site of these things, but they just leave me heartsick. The self-declared artist style themselves the intransigents, the impressionists; they take canvas, paint, and brushes, throw some color on at random, and sign the result" Albert Wolff, 1876 pg.2

"The unhappy impressionists can protest that his sincerity is absolute… But the public and the critics condemn him…. For them, only one fact pertains: the things that the impressionists put on their canvases do not correspond to those found on the canvases of previous painters. It is different, and so it is bad." - Theodore Duret, 1878 pg. 2

(Pg. 10 subtitle) **New Science, New Paint**
"France in the 18th century was in the forefront of the Age of Enlightenment, a time when a superstition was being replaced by the application of reason. At the same time, the machine age was sweeping Europe, what we call now the Industrial Revolution. Nearly every aspect of life was affected. Rational

thinking and industrial application gave rise to possibly the most important event in the history of science, the birth of modern chemistry. There were major leaps in the understanding of chemical interaction and the identification of basic elements. Previous to the year 1700 and 1850, 40, new elements were discovered!

The new chemical scientists were hired by industrial businesses such as textile manufacturers to find new and better ways to add color to their products. Brightly colored commodities sold better and for higher prices in the burgeoning market of cheap industrial manufactured goods. New substances were quickly investigated for their potential as pigments. Between 1800 and 1870 more than 20 intense yellow, green, blue, red and orange pigments were invented, many based on newly discovered elements such as chrome, cadmium, and cobalt. Each new pigment was quickly picked up by artist's colourmen, turned into paint, and sold to artists. New materials often gave an artist an opportunity for innovation, but this expansion in the number and variety of pigments was unprecedented in the history of art. An equally dramatic shift in the history of painting was bound to happen.

As a rule, the new pigments were more opaque and had greater tinting strength than traditional pigments. While some new pigments were only marginally better than similar traditional hues, others represented dramatic improvements, or were completely without precedent. Natural ultramarine blue was unrivaled in 600 years of art in terms of beauty and chemical stability. It was also enormously expensive, which limited its use. The new chemically identical 'French' ultramarine was dramatically cheaper, a tenth the cost, and could now be afforded by even the poorest painter. Chrome yellow was the first rich opaque yellow, that wasn't rare, expensive, highly toxic, or faded quickly in light. There had never been a strong, chemically stable green. Now there were three: chrome oxide green, emerald green, and viridian."

If you take a further look at the dress in our painting, (done in the spring of 1871) we have the experimentation of the well-known technique Monet used, wet-into-wet. We have, white painted wet canvas surface with added dabs of blue and pink mixed together lightly on canvases to form this style.

Approximately one year later, Monet, now at his house in Argenteuil (in the spring of 1872) perfected this technique in his painting, *Springtime*. So as you can see, the technique wet-into-wet didn't suddenly just occur, nor did the use of multiple colors. Our painting was a forerunner in the use of these techniques.

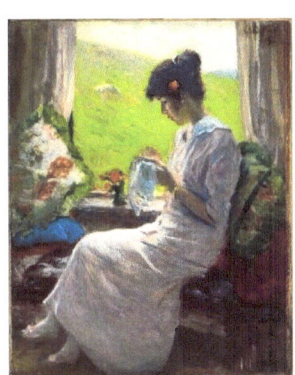 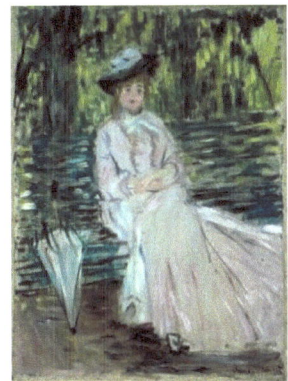 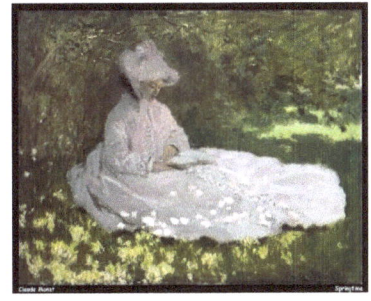

The Ladies in Pink Dresses

Paul Hayer Tuckers reference to the painting Springtime in his book (Claude Monet Life and Art) pg. 63 could apply to all three of these painting by Monet.

"Although his beautiful wife sits angelically on a carpet of green grass absorbed in her book, virtually every stroke on the canvas refuses to be integrated into the kind of polished whole that an audience of the 1870's would have expected from a finished picture. Camille's gown and bonnet, for example, are a collection of separate strokes of pink, lavender, and soft white while her face and hands are devoid of halftones."

All three works depict Monet's famous wet-in-wet technique.

Monet painted approximately 2000 oil paintings recorded in the Wildenstein Catalogue raisonne, which leads me to wonder where the incomplete paintings are? Many of Monet's paintings owned by collectors, and in museums today were intended to be preparatory paintings or sketches for future paintings. In the 1870s, artists experienced new innovations in art materials which differed from the previous 300 years. They were also seeing a major shift in the 200 years of artistic control by the government. Monet and the Impressionists found themselves to be living in the birth of the science and Industrial Revolution in 18th century Europe. Between 1800 and 1870, 20 intense yellows, greens, blues, reds, and orange pigments were invented and these new paints and canvases enabled them to experiment and change the art world of their time.

The 1860s and 1870s experienced a revolution in fine art paintings. New colors now came in tin tubes compressing paint and oil binders, spurring even more experimentation of the great outdoors. Monet's paintings in the late 1860s contained as many as 15 pigments in one painting; half of them traditional pigments. A decade later, at the height of pure Impressionism, their paintings generally contained no more than 8-10 pigments.

Duane R. Chartier's, Authentication Science and Art at Odds
"Great problems arise when the curatorial community is asked to consider works that do not easily "fit" into a neat art historical period or stylistic pigeonhole. Connoisseurs often will only accept the best works of an artist and discount inevitable products of the artist's evolution--- less accomplished works." Scientific principles and technical evidence can and must be used in order to elevate the practice of authentication."

Dr. Chartier, upon an examination of our painting made these observations:

- Overall, the paint is applied in long bold strokes.
- The signature was applied sometime after the original work had been completed.
- The thickness of paint on the facial area, is much thinner than on the remainder of the painting, indicating the pronounced knowledge of the subject matter.

Chapter 5
Monet's Sketchbook

In the book by Professor John House of the Cortland Institute, 'Monet, Nature into Art' pg.228 in the section appendix A: Monet's Drawing, their is a pencil drawing in one of the Eight Sketchbooks by Claude Monet, which survived.

Professor House explains that these were his rapid pencil sketches executed in notebooks as preliminary notations of possible sites or compositions for paintings. The drawings in these books shed considerable light on Monet's process of visualizing his subjects since they have been little discussed. A brief indication of their content is necessary in order to assess their likely functions. It is sometimes difficult to establish the starting date of a book because Monet seems to have chosen at random the pages he used rather than working consecutively through a book. At times he even used the reverse sides of certain pages, but at other times seems to have worked in an approximate reverse sequence, starting from the back.

Professor House continues-Pg. 228-229

[1] Inventory no. 5128, 26 X 34 cm. began c. 1865. Woman at a Window looking out over houses at the Sea; study for comparison of Dejeuner sur l'herbe; the placing of the drawings on P.I, very similar in style to the D'ejeuner study, suggests that it is a close to it in date, but perhaps predates it; P.I is an interesting comparison with Whistler's The Balcony, largely painted in 1865; various drawings of coastal scenes, including Etretat and probably F'ecamp, perhaps all of c.1865/ 69 [the drawings of F'ecamp reproduced in Seitz 1960, fig.75, may well have belonged with these; many pages in this book have been torn out]; <u>four Dutch scenes</u> of canals and windmills, presumably from Zaandam in 1871 [<u>one rep. Tucker 1982, pl. 34</u>; the presence of Dutch subjects suggest that this book also accompanied Monet to London in 1870, 71;]

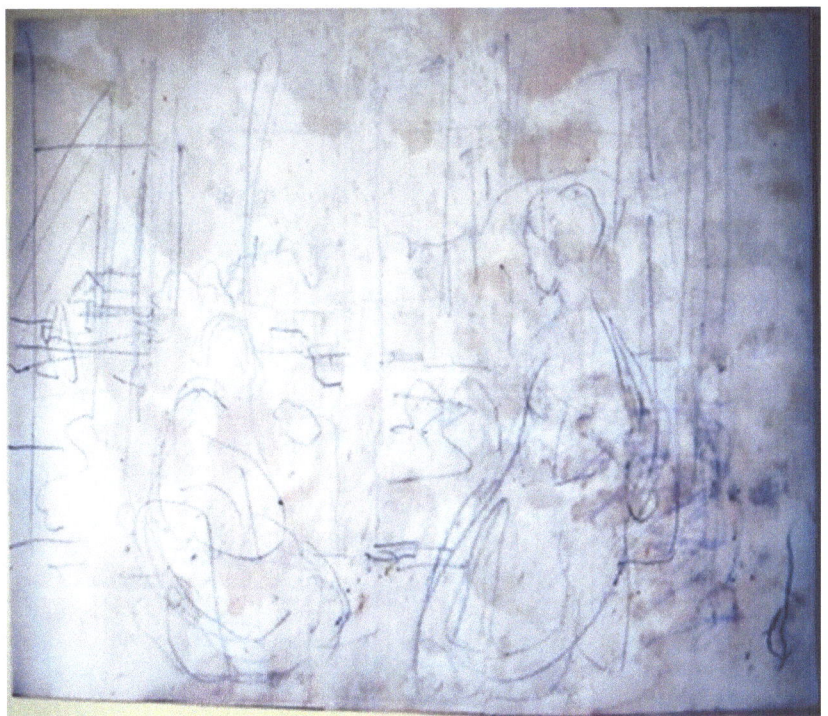

Many of Monet's sketches have been attributed to his paintings. Some believe this sketch to be linked to the 1865 Luncheon in the Grass series. However, there are others who believe this sketch, due to the Dutch scenes of canals and windmills, was done in Zaandam, Holland while Monet and Camille visited in 1871.

At the Musse Marmottan, you can view the Monet sketchbooks.

Sketchbook number one on page one

This sketchbook (Marmottan inventory number 5128) is large and formatted, with covers measuring 263 x 352 mm. It contains 34 extent sheets. There is evidence that the book originally contained at least 52 sheets as stubs of 18 torn out pages remain.

Monet made use of this album sporadically over the course of more than 50 years, starting in Fontainebleau and Normandy during the mid-1860s, in London and Holland 1871, contueing Paris in the 1870s, and even at Giverny 1910s.

It contains studies related to his paintings, Luncheon On the Grass - 1865, the Gare Sant-Lazare series 1877, and Water Lilies c. 1914 – 1919, in addition to a sequence of portraits of the artists, children and stepchildren c. 1885. Several of the water-lily studies are executed in violet crayon.

Go to book 1, Page 1. of the museums site, In the notes located at the info. button, on the bottom of the page is written:
"In opposition to Wildenstein and House Bouldewijn Bakker suggests Holland, 1871 for the drawing's location and date."

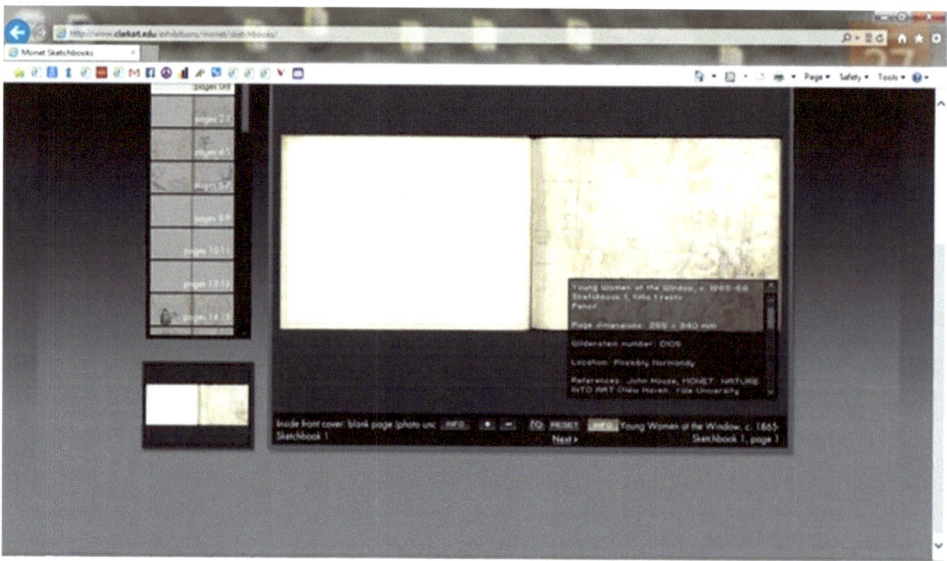

We believe our painting is a product of Monet's sketchbook Book 1, page 1, inventory number 5128 and we agree with Tucker and Boudewijn Bakkers suggestion of the drawing's location and date of 1871 Zaandam, Holland which is consistent with the date of 1871 on our painting.

Here is the description that is given of the sketch in Professor House's book Nature into Art , "Woman at a window looking out over houses and the sea," and "these were rapid pencil sketches executed in notebooks, as preliminary notations of possible sites of compositions for paintings."

For the first time there is a painting to form a comparison with the sketch. Both, show a woman sitting next to a window with curtains near her back, and towards the front. Both have a windowsill line and have a landscape horizon line.

The description Professor House gives, is of 'a woman looking out over the sea'. The sea line in the painting is to the far uper right, behind the woman's head. Monet decided not to add houses to this painting. He treated the background as he did number of years later when he painted 'Camille holding a Posey of violets.'

To summarize, the sketch with no definitive painting assigned to compare a resemblance, it could or might be argued to have been made from the 1865 Luncheon on the Grass series. However, now we have a sketch and painting with simuler appearances, a woman sitting surrounded by curtains and many other similarities and comparisons.

Both the painting and sketch resemble one another.

Well, so much for the sketch in Monet's own Sketchbooks. At this point, I had learned that Monet left behind his accounting books. I researched where they may have been located and set out to find them.

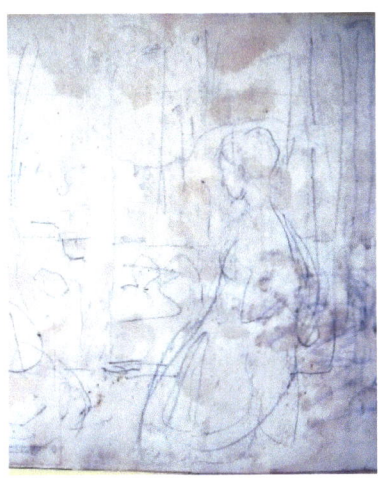 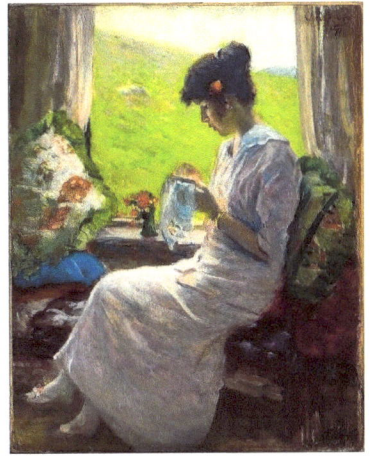

Chapter 6
Monet's Account Books & Auction

Back in the 1960s-1980s, it would have been impossible for my father to have researched this painting as I have been able to in this day and age. The instant nature of today's internet makes a significant difference, as information is now available which could not be readily accessed in the past. Records kept in old ledgers are being photographed, translated and are available for viewing. As long as you are patient and ask for help, you will meet a lot of good and helpful people. In fact, my niece currently works for a company that converts old paper documents into researchable online material. Now, not only art experts have the ability to research information, therefore making it easier for the rest of us to be able to research thoroughly and come to our own conclusions.

In January 2012, my wife (whose help has been invaluable in this process) and I ordered Monet's accounting books. The Musse Marmottan was so kind to have e-mailed to us Monet's accounting records which spanned years 1872 - 1875. A record of sale which came to my attention, was dated November 23, 1872. This was a painting that Monet had sold to Paul Durand-Ruel for 400 francs named, Figure in Rose. I researched further and found out that it had been renamed, The Reader, then renamed once more to the painting we now know today as Springtime.

This painting currently resides at Walters Art Museum. I visited their website and examined both the painting and its provenance. I noticed the provenance on their website did not match the provenance in the 1996 Wildenstein Catalogue Raisonne that I happened to have. We emailed Jo Briggs at the museum and made a few inquiries. The reply received was short and sweet, "It came from the Catalogue Raisonne, Daniel Wildenstein, did in 1974."

Let me try to describe for you the 1996 catalogue. It consists of 4 books app 10x13 inches each, and in total are about 5-1/2 to 6 inches thick. Volume 1 is Danial's story of Claude Monet's life. Volume 2-3-and 4, lists Monet's paintings. Each painting has a photograph and assigned a number and any exhibitions are listed along with a bibliography, a brief commentary and a Provenance.

What is Provenance you ask?

Provenance (taken from the French *provenir* which means "to come from"), is the chronology of the ownership, custody or location of a historical object. The term was originally used in relation to works of art, but is now used in a similar sense within a wide range of fields including: archaeology, paleontology, archives, manuscripts, printed books and science computing.

The primary purpose of tracing the provenance of an object or entity is normally to provide contextual and circumstantial evidence for its original production or discovery by establishing its history; especially through a sequence of its formal ownership, custody and places of storage. The practice has a particular value in helping to authenticate objects.

Comparative techniques, expert opinions and the results of scientific tests may also be used to these ends, but establishing provenance is essentially a matter of documentation."

The reason I put the definition of the word 'Provenance' here is also because it is the bench mark the art word requires and is the guideline of what I must accomplish. I will try to provide contextual and circumstantial evidence for our paintings origin, production and discovery. Also, I as far as practical provide its later history, especially a sequence of its former ownership, custody and places of storage. Each painting Monet did has its own provenance and is unique into itself or each is different.

Lets go back to the 1974 Catalogue.

Daniel in his 1974 Catalogue Raisonne of Claude Monet's paintings catalogued all the known Monet paintings and their histories into books.

This is the 1974 provenance displayed in 2012, at Walters Art Museums website on their painting 'Springtime.' (They changed it after I brought this to their attention)

Provenance [Problematic history prior to when Henry Walters acquired painting, [Either] Sale [by artist], Hotel Drouot, Paris, February 4, 1873 no. 55 [as Jeune femme assises]; Paul Durand Ruel [by purchase;] [Or] Sale [by artist] November, 1872; Paul Durand –Ruel [by purchase] and resold before 1877, as la femme en rose] Hoschrde, Paris; [Either] Hoschede Sale, Hotel Drouot Paris June 5 –6, 1878 no. 54 [as Jeune femme assise dan un parc]; Lussac (?);[or] Hoschede Sale 1881 –1888 [50 francs] [as Femme assise dans l'herbe]; Paul Durand Ruel; Mary Cassatt, 1889; Henry Walters, Baltimore, May 7, 1903 by purchase [George a Lucas as agent]; Walters's art Museum, 1931 by bequest.

William R. Johnston, in his book 'The Nineteenth Century Paintings in the Walters Art Gallery' pg. 142, made note of Daniels reconstruction of the provenance or imposing the '1873 account of sale', on a painting that was sold in 1872."

Here is the provenance that was done approximately 22 years later in Daniel Wildensteins <u>1996</u> Catalogue Raisonne of Springtime's provenance. [This would include the 1974 paintings plus any new discoveries between 74-96.]

PROVENANCE

Probably purchased from Monet by Paul Durand Ruel on 23 November 1872 (Figure in Rose) and Sold to Ernest Hoschede on 28 April 1873. Sale Hoschede, Paris Drouot 5-6 June, 1878 no. 54 (lussac) Mary Cassatt Paris's. c. 1889 Henry Walters.1903 currently at the Walters art Gallery Baltimore, Maryland.''

This is what was **removed** from the 1974 Wildenstein Catalogue Raisonne, when the 1996 Catalogue Raisonne was published:

Sale [by artist], Hotel Drouot Paris February 4, 1873 no. 55 [as Jeune femme assise]; Paul Durand Ruel, [by purchase.] (A young woman sitting)

So you can see that their are two different paintings in the 1974 version, November 23, 1872 and Febuary 4,1873. In the 1996, their is one.

Flavie Durand-Ruel is the custodian of Paul Durand-Ruel's records. We made an inquiry as to Daniel Wildenstein's reference to the Feb. 4, 1873 auction sale in Springtime's provenance. She confirmed:

'Durand Ruel bought at public auction in Paris at Drouot on February 4, 1873, Oudard auctioneer, O'Doard expert:
Lot No.55 by Claude Monet 'Femme assise.'
However, neither in the sale catalogue, nor in our books, do we have any further information regarding this 'Femme assise' : we neither have it's dimensions, nor it's history after this purchase. Unfortunately at this time,

our archives have some lacks."

Flavie Durand-Ruel relayed to us that their records are lacking in regards to the purchases of the painting that Paul purchased on February 4, 1873, number 55. It seems that both seller and buyer did not place much value on the painting at the time of sale, and that the buyer was not encouraged to or did not treat the painting with a great deal of importance or significance.

I wanted to review the records from the Hotel Drouot auction. I found that the old Drouot Hotel Auctions' sales records were at the INHA or the National Institute for Art History Library. After inquiring, we received an email from Chantal Georgel.

"Title catalog of modern paintings, watercolors and drawings, marble, terra-cotta, sale/Drouot/February 4, 1873, second bathroom, Charles Oudart auctioneer, O`Dorard- expert. No 55: Monet (Claude) jeune femme assise."

William R. Johnston in his book "The Nineteenth Century Paintings in the Walters Art Gallery" page 142, made note of Daniels reconstruction of the provenance.

"Provenance The painting was purchased from Mary Cassatt together with the Degas Portrait of a woman for a combined price of 25,000 francs by George A. Lucas acting as agent for Henry Walters on May 7, 1903 (Lucas Diary 2: 914; The previous history of the picture is problematical. D. Wildenstein reconstructs its provenance as follows: ''Either, Sale (Monet) Hotel Drouot, Paris, February 4, 1873, no. 55 (Jeune femme assise) to Durand-Ruel: or, bought from Monet by Durand-Ruel, November 1872 and resold before 1877

(La femme en rose''; Hoschede, Paris; either, Sale (Hoschede) Hotel Drouot, Paris June 5-6, 1878, no. 54 (Jeune femme assise dans un pare) to lussac (?) or, bought at Hoschede in 1881 for 50 francs by Durand-Ruel and resold by Durand-Ruel between 1884-1888 (Femme assise dans l'herbe) and bought by Mary Cassatt about 1889; Henry Walters, 1903.''

In 2014 I was in communication with Mare-Christine Maufus of the Wildenstein Institute, France. I asked her why Daniel Wildenstein added to Springtimes provenance the painting 'A Young Woman Sittimg' in his 1974 Catalogue Raisonne and in his 1996 version he had it removed? She said ``In the 1996 revised edition catalog, Daniel Wildenstein took into account the information published in 1980, in the exhibition Homage to Claude Monet'' [The 1980 book, Homage to Claude Monet pg. 118]

They removed the painting from Springtimes provenance but, I would still like an answer to my question , as to why another painting was ever put in Springtimes provenance? Also, after it was removed, what happened to this painting ? I searched, but found no other accounting of this painting. I compiled a list of paintings Monet did of Camille before Febuary 4th, 1873. I found seventeen and all have provenances that are complete, with no mention of this auction date.

Here is a list of Monet paintings that featured Camille or of a woman sitting painted before February 4, 1873. Note that all have provenance which are complete, with no mention of February 4, 1873 no.55.

Beach at Trouville - Painted in 1870. Sold in 1920 to Alphonse Kann. Two women with umbrellas.
On the Beach at Trouville - Painted 1870. Purchased from Monet by Paul

Durand Ruel, in June 1871 and sold during the exhibition in London. Present location unknown.

Camille Sitting on the Beach at Trouville - Painted in 1870. Purchased from Monet by critic Emile Belmont, 1875.

Camille on the Beach at Trouville - Painted in 1870. Purchased from Monet by Martin, in 1874 or 1875.

Camille on the Beach - Painted in 1870. Michael Monet, Giverny Bequeathed in 1966 to the Academe des Beaux-Arts, Paris currently in the Musee Marmottan, Paris.

On the Beach of Trouville - Painted in 1870. Michael Monet, Giverny.

Meditation, Mrs. Monet Sitting on a Sofa - Painted in 1871, London. Monet sold his painting [La Lecture] to Paul Durand Ruel in 1873 and resold to the Princes De Monbeliard in 1889.

Springtime (The Reader) - Painted in 1872. Purchased from Monet by Paul Durand Ruel in November, 1872 and sold Hoschede in April 1873.

The Red Kerchief, Portrait of Ms. Monet - Painted in 1873. Monet never sold.

Camille in the Garden with Jean and his Nanny - Painted in 1873. Purchased from Monet by Jean Baptise Faure, Paris, 1874.

The Bench - Painted in 1873. Cassirer, Berlin Ed. Arnhold Berlin, 1909.

Camille and Jean Monet in the Garden at Argenteuil - Painted in 1873. Michael Monet, Giverny.

Camille Monet at the Window - Painted in 1873. Michael Monet, Giverny.

Woman Sitting on a Beach - Painted in 1874, and purchased by Pascal, Paris in 1877 (this canvas shows a model who posed for Degas and other artists)

Camille Embroidering - Painted in 1875. Sale Monet, Morisot, Renoir and Sisley, Paris, Drouot, 24 March 1875.

The Walk, Woman with a Parasol - Painted in 1875.

Camille Monet and a Child in the Garden - Painted in 1875

With the records from the Drouot Auction, and Paul Durant-Ruel purchase, along that it is mentioned in the 1974 Wildenstein Catalogue Raisonne, it is safe to conclude that there is a (now known) Claude Monet painting Missing!

We believe we have that painting and its based on a host of researched information to include a list of convincing comparisions, and a hard to obtain, positive letter from Walter McCrone of the McCrone Research Institute. The provenance. is better then most of Monet's paintings.

Chapter 7
The Provenance

I will attempt to stay within the boundary of the definition of provenance and to provide contextual and circumstantial evidence for our painting's origin, production and discovery because it is the benchmark that the art world requires and they should not expect otherwise.

We know about my father's discovery in 1962. We also know about the McCrone report and Dr. Ashok Roy's bulletins 5 & 6 at The National Gallery in London which Dr. McCrone used to compare our painting's brushstrokes, first use of paints, and the mixing of colors. Additionally, we compiled lists of comparisons and similarities to other paintings of Camille, by Monet.

We have a sketch that is in one of the sketchbooks that accompanied Monet to Holland which resembles our painting. This was found in John Houses book, Nature into Art where he refers to it as, Woman at a Window Looking out over Houses and Sea. Our painting features the curtains, similar dress and a woman with her hair worn up and even out of the window a small glance of the sea can be seen.

We know about the painting Monet sold on February 4, 1973 no 55. to Paul Durand-Ruel. We also know that in the 1974 Wildenstein Catalogue Raisonne of Monets Painting the 1973 auction sale date painting was inserted into the provenance of the painting Springtime, with the sale date of November 23rd of 1872.

Our painting was tested by Walter McCrone of the McCrone Institute where it was found that the paint is of Monet's time and of his palette. The mixing of colors is as Monet mixed paint. The brushstrokes were examined, and Dr. McCrone utilized Dr. Ashok Roy's bulletins from the National Gallery London to compare. Dr. McCrone also made this statement:

"Everything we have seen and done agree remarkably well with the known palette of Claude Monet. I see no reason to doubt the attribution to one of my favorite artists Claude Monet."

We know that a painting by Claude Monet exists, named *'A Young Woman Sitting'*, and that it was sold at auction, by Monet, in Paris, on February 4, 1873.

We know it was sold to Paul Durand-Ruel, who because of the unpopularity of impressonist painting in France at the time, shipped many of the impressionist paintings to his gallery in London.

We know that my father's painting was purchased in 1962 and is of `A Young Woman Sitting' with the date of 1871, and a signature of Claude Monet.

We know that Paul Durand-Ruel purchased a painting called, A Young Woman Sitting from Claude Monet at a Paris auction, and thereafter it was probably shipped to his London gallery named, The German Gallery.

Ancestral records show that in 1847, Frederick W. Wildenstein, a German in London, attended his sons wedding, Friedrich Heinrich Otto Wildenstein.
The census records for 1870 and 1880 from The United States Department of Interior National Parks Service Fort Union National Monument Santa Fe National Historal Trail Watrus New Mexico and the Old Watrus Cemertery show both Carl, and Frederick Wildenstein in the Watrus New Mexico area.

The 1871 books of Marriage show the marriage of Carl W. Wildenstein's to Belina Watrus, in Watrus New Mexico. The Mora County Census of 1870s show a 29 yr.old Carl Wildenstein. The 1880 census show a 38 yr. old Carl Wildenstein and family including a 80yr old Carl Wildenstein. They missnamed the 80yr old Wildenstein. The Old Watrus Cemetary records show him as Frederick W Wildenstein Engineer died in 1896 at 88yrs old.

Frederick Wildenstein a german while in London would naturally be drawn to a german gallery, where he purchased the painting and it remained as part of his household possessions when he joined his son Carl in New Mexico in the late 1870s.

In my conversations with Jim Abteu, who is a desendent of Carl Wildenstein's daughter Johanna Wildenstein, said he remmbers as a boy the very room the painting was displayed.

This practice of shipping paintings to London by Paul Durand-Ruel is confirmed by <u>Daniel Wildenstein</u>, in his 1996 Claude Monet Catalogue Raisonne, volume 1 on page 99 under the title INCOME it says, "The year 1872 was remarkable not only for its (extent) production but for the income that this production generated. Monet sold five pictures to Latouch, two to Millot, one to his brother, Leon, and one to Edouard Manet; but his best client by far was Paul Durand Ruel, who bought a significant number of paintings and continue to exhibit Monet in his exhibitions in <u>London</u>." Pg 100, Speaking of 1873 as a good year for Monet mostly because Durand-Ruels lion's share of his purchases, Durand-Ruel fell victim of a brief recession in France. In 1872-1873 he was losing clientele because of his commitment to avant-garde paintings. Paintings were shipped to London, to a better market.

Let us summarize this information and its probable conclusions.

1871 - Monet in Holland did a sketch; John House calls it, young woman at a window looking out over houses and the sea. The Musse Marmottan refers to it as, young woman at the window.

1871 - Monet in Holland painted A Young Woman Sitting, dated 1871.

1873 - Claude Monet sold his painting A Young Woman Sitting, to Paul Durand-Ruel.

1873 – 1880 - Frederick W. Wildenstein, a German engineer living in London, purchased Monet's painting, A Young Woman Sitting from the German Gallery, owned by Paul Durand-Ruel before he joined his son in Watrous, New Mexico.

1962 - Under horrific circumstances, Ernest Wildenstein a resident of Las Vegas, New Mexico, sold the painting A Young Woman Sitting with the date of 1871 and signature of Claude Monet to Virgil Haverstick Sr.

2000 - The painting, A Young Woman Sitting is confirmed by the McCrone Institute to be by the artist, Claude Monet.

2000 - From a photograph, Daniel Wildenstein turned down the authentication of the Haverstick painting.

2010 - 2016 - The provenance has been established by the Haverstick family for the painting 'A Young Woman Sitting'.

PROVENANCE

Timeline of ownership of Claude Monet's painting "A young woman sitting"

Owner	Years Owned	Total Yrs.
Claude Monet	1871 – 1872	2 years
Paul Durand–Ruel	1873 – 1880	8 years
Frederick Wildenstein	1881 – 1889	9 years
Carl Wildenstein	1890 – 1896	7 years
Belinda Wildenstein	1897 – 1924	27 years
Lewis Wildenstein	1925 – 1957	32 years
Ernest Wildenstein	1958 – 1962	5 years
Virgil Haverstick Sr.	1963 – 2005	42 years
Virgil Haverstick Jr.	2006 – 2019	13 years
		Total 145 years

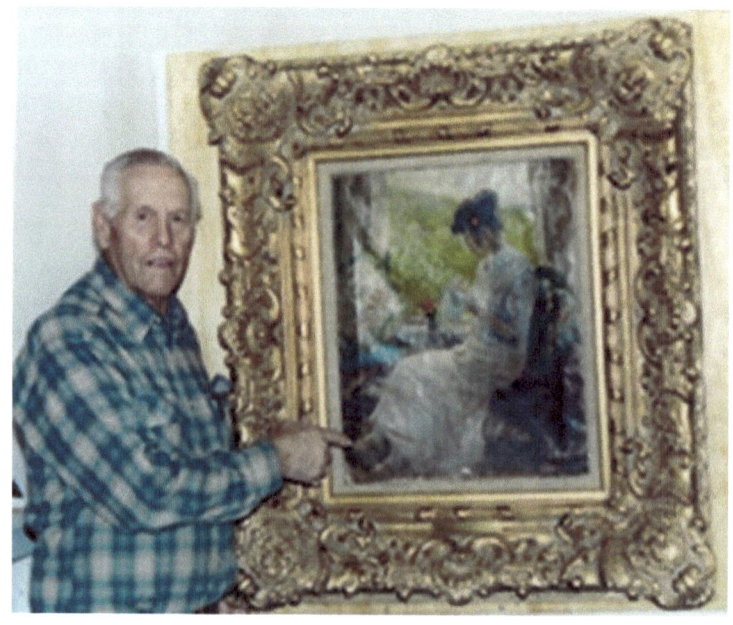

Virgil Haverstick Sr. and his Claude Monet Paintimg.

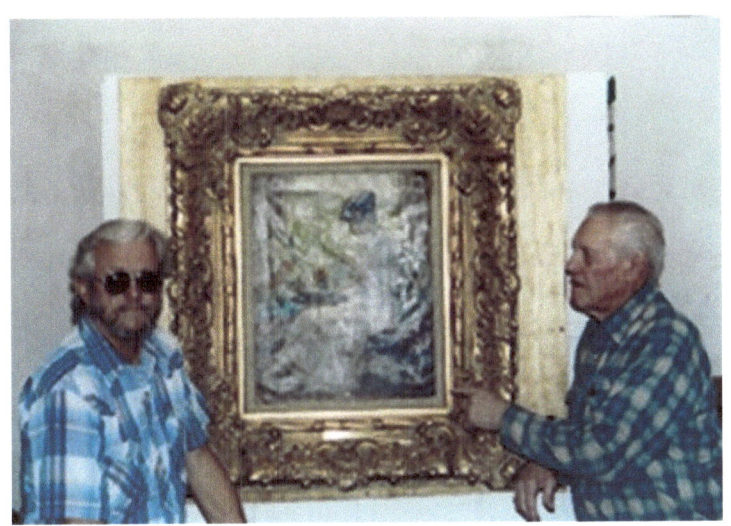
Me with my Dad

We are fortunate the painting is still with us today. It once had a beautifue ornate frame, that was stolen. The thief kicked out the painting and left it on the floor face down. It turned out that a few years later their was a fire in dads studio. The unframed painting wrapped in a thick Navajo blanket survived the fire. If not for a thiefs intervention the painting would probably have perished.

Conclusion
Chapter 8

I have well established that there is a painting of Camille 'A Young Woman Sitting' that is missing. Monet painted her in 1871 and he took her to the Drouot Auction on February 4th, 1873. Art dealer and Galley owner Paul Durand-Ruel, a little over two months earlier, November 72 bought the painting 'Springtime' and several other paintings from Monet, but on this day, he was working as the art expert for the auction house. Auction records show that Monet sold his painting, and Paul's records show it went to his gallery as a purchase.

A hundred years later in 1974, it is mentioned in Daniel Wildenstein's Catalogue Raisonne when he put it in the provenance of another painting named Springtime. In the 1980s book 'Homage to Claude Monet' it was decided it should be removed. Another mention was the William R. Johnston book, 'The Nineteenth Century Paintings in the Walters Art Gallery 'where he brings to our attention of Daniel's reconstruction of Springtime's provenance.

In 1962, the painting appears once more. In Albuquerque New Mexico, a family by the name of Wildenstein were going through a horrifying family experience. They called my father to examine an assortment of old paintings for sale. They were trying to raise money to pay for funeral and hospital expenses, for a car-truck accident that took the lives of almost an entire family. Dad bought fifteen paintings. A while later he noticed that one painting had a signature of Claude Monet 71. He was not that familiar with this artist, so he showed the painting to several art galleries in the Santa Fe art community.
 Many years passed, and he decided to find out once and for all if his painting was truly a Monet. He sought after the best in The McCrone Institute and Dr. Walter McCrone. Dr McCrone enlisted the best in Dr. Askok Roy, the Director

of Scientific Research at the National Gallery in London. The McCrone Institute had it for several months and it passed all tests, it was determined to be an authentic Claude Monet painting.

Dad was excited, but it didn't take long for him to learn that Daniel Wildenstein must first approve of its authenticity. Dad died in 2005, still trying to prove to the Wildenstein Institute that it was authentic.

Years later, I thought I would see if there was anything I could do. I caught up on his research and read my father's old books on Monet. I ordered several more and found a sketch in one of Monet's old Sketchbooks that resembled our painting. Next, I ordered Monet's old account books and found that there is indeed a painting named `A Young Woman Sitting,' missing. I learned about the 1974 and 1996 catalogue incident regarding the painting Springtime and determined that our painting is indeed the painting that was sold in 1873

There are many missing paintings in the world. That is why there are those that are trusted to uncover the fake paintings and display to us, the public, the authentic works of an artist. What do you do if you find an old painting with a signature of a well-known artist? You hope the catalogue holder of that artist is an honest organization. Only then can you say that your find will be amongst other authentic works.

The Wildenstein Plattner Institute is now in charge of receiving any newly discovered or lost paintings of Claude Monet. The head of research is Pascal Perrin. If you have questions or additional research to assist Mr. Perrin I am sure he would love to hear for you. [pascal.perrin@wpi.art]

Anyone who really studies my research will believe as I do, that we have indeed found the missing Claude Monet painting, 'A Young Woman Sitting.'

About the Author

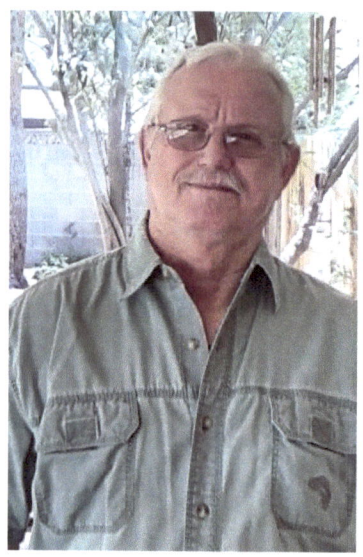

I was born in Texas, raised in New Mexico and lived in California. I am now retired and reside in Las Vegas, Nevada with my wife Cathy. After working in construction most of my life here is my attempt to write a book about my family's painting.

If you have additional information to add, correspondence should be addressed to virgilhaverstick@gmail.com

www.ingramcontent.com/pod-product-compliance
Lightning Source LLC
Chambersburg PA
CBHW051204220526
45473CB00003B/900